A Little Book of Klezmer Fiddle Tunes

30 tunes that are fun to play for all fiddlers!

Collected & edited by
JM Bolton

Fat Pony Music Books
a division of
International Digital Book Publishing Industries - USA

Copyright © 2020 Johanna M Bolton

All rights reserved.
Except for the inclusion of brief quotations in a review, no part of this book may be reproduced by any means electronic, mechanical, photocopy, recording, or otherwise without written permission from the author or publisher.
While the arrangements in this book are, as much as possible, originals, the songs themselves are in the public domain and having made the previous statement to satisfy the lawyers, have fun with the songs and do whatever you have to within the limits of your conscience.

Published by

 Fat Pony Music – a division of IDBPI

Additional copies of this book, or other titles by JM BOLTON are available online
(Amazon.com)
or contact the author at
fatponymusic52@yahoo.com

ISBN 978-1-57550-095-9

Fat Pony Music - International Digital Book Publishing Industries

Printed in the United States of America
Design, layout, formatting by JM Bolton

10 9 8 7 6 5 4 3 2 1

Some reviews for Bolton's music books:

Play It Now! - Met all my expectations. You can start playing and enjoying your instrument right out of the box. Music should be fun. This book makes sure you do. Well pleased.

A Psaltery Christmas - Lovely book for the bowed psaltery, or any treble instrument. All of the songs were chosen with the desire by the author to "capture the essence of traditional Christmas." There is a section of "Notes" telling the story/history/lore/and personal thoughts and memories of each song. Each piece is presented with the main melody and a duet counterpart (as opposed to merely a harmony part). A book I know I am going to love and refer to often. The author has done equally enchanting work in her other books, "Early Music" and "20 Celtic Tunes"

Psaltery Players rejoice! Very good music book for the psaltery or other treble instrument. The music is easy to read and also gives each note by name to help those who aren't music reader. And chords are also given for added enrichment. Bolton has collected a very nice book full of Celtic tunes here. I have really enjoyed playing songs from this book on my psaltery.

Early Music – Lovely collection of early music, divided into time periods from the 13th century through the 18th century. Each song has the main tune and additional staves for secondary parts for the bowed psaltery and other treble instruments.

Five stars! Informative and nice Early Music book. Satisfied buyer with this one! I love this music book and was even more excited about it once I looked through the content. It has some absolutely great information as well as easy to follow sheet music.

Great book! Took it to my ensemble group and we used it for violin, harp and psaltery - great choices over the centuries.

Five stars - I really like the ease of reading this music. Glad I bought this.

Five Stars - Shows why the bowed psaltery is perfect for medieval hymns

*Hand-colored papercut - early 20th century
by an unknown artist.*

Note from the author:

Klezmer is a Yiddish word that means *music*. But you don't have to be Jewish to appreciate klezmer. There is something about these tunes that awakens an almost uncontrollable desire to dance! Klezmer does that.

Klezmer is thought to originate with the Ashkenazi Jews of Eastern Europe. Originally the music consisted of dance tunes and pieces for weddings and other celebrations. Compared with most other European folk-music styles, little is known about the history of klezmer. There is, however, a heavy influence of Romani music, since many Jews and Roma lived side by side in Europe.

It is important to realize that the written notes are only an approximation of how the music should sound. Like Celtic music, klezmer is all about individual expression and ornamentation. Because of this, you should introduce any ornamentation you feel is appropriate. It's up to you, the musician, to interpret the songs, and if you play klezmer only as written, you are not really playing klezmer at all. Experiment and have fun!

A note on speed: Playing fast? No, no, and no. You are going to hear musicians famous for being able to play extremely fast, and I won't blame you for thinking, "I'll never be able to do that!" Well, why would you want to? Playing music that fast is just showing off. You can't dance to it. You can't sing it. And you really can't enjoy the music if it goes by like an express train! So, don't worry about playing fast or even playing to speed. Just enjoy yourself making music.

Along with most aspects of European Jewish culture klezmer was almost lost forever because of the Holocaust. Like most folk music, klezmer is an aural tradition, passed on from musician to musician. When the older musicians died, their music died with them. The very few who survived have helped to revitalize the music along with musicologists who have worked tirelessly to record their repertoires.

I'm not going to pretend to be an authority on klezmer and so I won't be taking up space with tips on ornamentation, bowing, or any of that. There is a glossary in the back of the book for reference as well as notes on the tunes and some ornamentation. I recommend listening to videos on YouTube to help you get a feel for the music.

The pieces in this book were selected because they are melodious and not overly complicated. In some cases I simplified the notation even further to make the music accessible to a beginning fiddler. My goal is to allow more people to appreciate this music.

The book is smaller than usual so it will fit into your fiddle case. You can use it on a music stand or leave it open on the floor as a quick reference when you are playing in a group.

One last thing - remember to play the *music* not just the notes. I'm going to say that again because it's very important: remember to play the *music* not just the notes. Try to get into the spirit of the tunes. But most of all, enjoy!

Enough words ... get out your fiddle, turn the page, and play some music!

Johanna M Bolton
August 2020

P.S. A note about the illustrations: the traditional Jewish art form of papercutting is relatively unknown today, however, the earliest reference dates to 1345. It was once a common art form as even the poorest Jew had access to paper. These papercuts feature most of the traditional symbols and inscriptions found in Jewish ceremonial objects and amulets. That so few of these items remain is not surprising considering how delicate they are. Also, the Holocaust marked the disappearance of much Jewish ceremonial and folk art, especially pieces as fragile as papercuts.

This book is for my Opa,
Richard Thierry Finck,
a wonderful pianist who performed in the early days of radio in New York with my Aunt Honey (a violinist), as well as patiently accompanying me when I was a fledgling fiddle player.

I remember working through my classical assignments until Opa became bored and started swinging the music to a ragtime beat. Frustrated, I would yell for Oma who would call back, "Richard! Play it nice!"

Richard did play it very nice, indeed. He shone at family parties, playing his repertory of popular 1920 and 30's tunes while everyone would gather around the old upright to sing and dance.

We had some good times …

Table of Contents

1 - Adir Hu
4 - Ale Brider
5 - Arabian Dance
6 - Around the Fire
7 - Ayli Lyuli
8 - Bulgar
9 - Chava
12 - Dan's Freilach
10 - Dona Dona
13 - Essen esst Zich
14 - Gypsy Bulgar
29 - Hava Nagila
15 - Heyser Bulgar
27 - Hopak Katsatske
16 - Klez
21 - Long Live the Negum
18 - Mazltov
2 - Night in the Garden of Eden
19 - Oh Yossel Yossel
20 – Oj Tate
21 - Papirosn
22 - Regndl
23 - Reina
24 - Shabes in Vilna
7 - Shalom Aleichem I
25 - Shalom Aleichem II
26 - Sher from Khevrisa
28 - Sherele

30 - More About the Music
30 - Glossary
32 - About the Author
32 - More Books

Adir Hu

A Night in the Garden of Eden
A Nacht in Gan Eydn

A Night in the Garden of Eden - continued

Ale Brider

Arabian Dance
Araber Tanz

Around the Fire

Arum dem Fayer

Ayli Lyuli

Shalom Aleichem 1

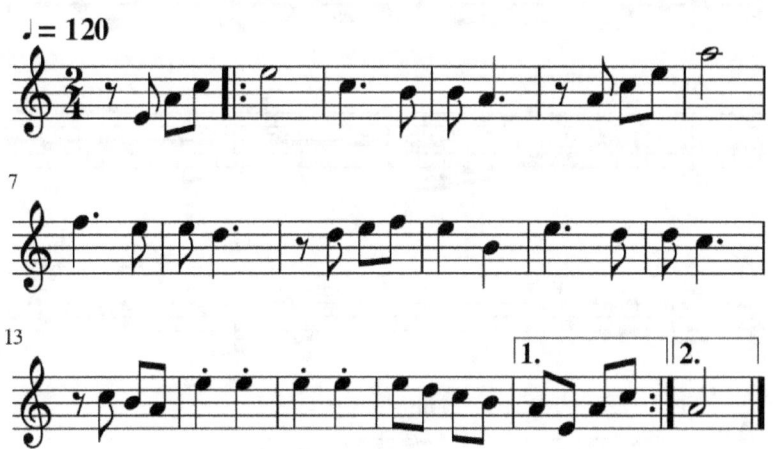

Bulgar

Chava

Dona Dona

Dona Dona – continued

1) On a wagon bound for market
   There's a calf with a mournful eye
   High above him there's a swallow
   Winging swiftly through the sky

Refrain 1 How the winds are laughing
   They laugh with all their might
   Laugh and laugh the whole day through
   And half the summer's night

2) "Stop complaining", said the farmer
   Who told you a calf to be?
   Why don't you have wings to fly with
   Like the swallow so proud and free?

   Refrain 1

Refrain 2 Dona, Dona, Dona, Dona,
   Dona, Dona, Dona, Dou,
   Dona, Dona, Dona, Dona,
   Dona, Dona, Dona, Dou

3) Calves are easily bound and slaughtered
   Never knowing the reason why
   But whoever treasures freedom
   Like the swallow has learned to fly

   Refrain
   Refrain 2

Dan's Freilach

Esssen esst Zich

Gypsy Bulgar

Heyser Bulgar

Klez

Long Live the Nigun (Music)

Mazltov

Oh Yossel Yossel

Oj Tate

Viktor Emil Frankl

Papirosn (Cigarettes)

Traditional Bulgarian Folk Tune

Regndl

Reina

Shabes in Vilna

♩ = 120

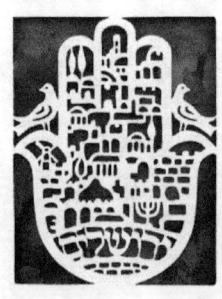

Shalom Aleichem - II

Sher from Khevrisa

Sher - continued

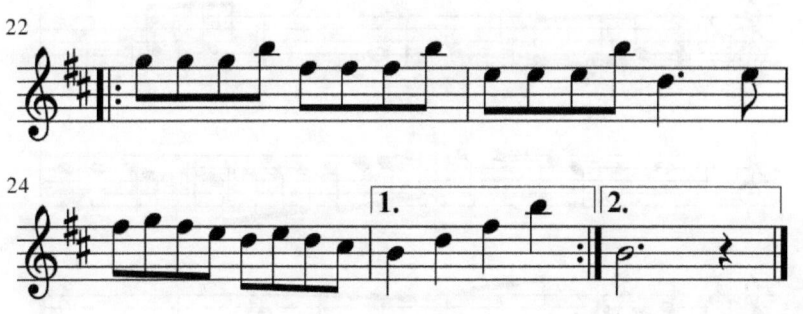

Hopak Katsatske

Sherele

Hava Nagila

More About the Music

Dona Dona (page 10) has become popular as a folk song, but was originally originally written for a play by Sholom Secunda and Aaron Zeitlin. It's a duet by a man and a woman, with each of them alternately singing the first refrain, and both singing the second together. There are several English translations, but this one by Arthur Kevess and Teddi Schwartz is the most popular.

Hava Nagila – page 31, (Hebrew: הבה נגילה, Havah Nagilah, "Let us rejoice") is an Israeli folk song, based on Psalm and traditionally sung at Jewish celebrations. The lyrics are based on Psalm 118 (verse 24) of the Hebrew Bible. The first commercial recording of the song was produced in Berlin in 1922.

Papirosn - page 22, This song tells the tale of an orphaned cigarette peddler freezing in the rain on a street corner. Papirosn long ago entered the folk tradition, with several variants. One is the doina or lament in Rumanian-Yiddish style; another is a rollicking dance-band version in Klezmer style.

Glossary

Bulgar (bulgarish) - dance from Bulgaria, but also can mean of Wallachian or Romani origin.

Csárdás - popular dance among Jews from Hungary, Slovakia and the Carpathians.

Doina is an improvisational lament usually performed solo. It is extremely important in weddings. Its basis is the Romanian shepherd's lament, so it has an expressive vocal quality.

Fantazi or fantasy is a freeform song, traditionally played at Jewish weddings as the guests dined. It resembles the fantasia of "light" classical music.

Freylekh (festive) - from the Romanian traditional song and dance

Hora (or **zhok**, which means *dance*) is a Romanian-style dance. The Israeli hora has its roots in the Romanian hora.
Khevrisa is a Yiddish term which usually refers to a talmudic study group. Back in the Old World, klezmorim adopted it into their slang as another reference for a music group.
Khosidl (or khusidl) - named after the Hasidic Jews who danced it, is a dignified embellished dance in 2/4 or 4/4 time. It is performed in either a circle or a line.
Klezmorim – musicians who play klezmer.
Kolomeike is a fast dance originating in Ukraine; is a prominent in the folk music of that country.
Mazltov, mazel tov - good wishes; Used to express congratulations or best wishes especially at weddings.
Mazurka and the **polka** - Polish and Czech dances, respectively.
Nigun - melody in both Yiddish and Hebrew. This is a moderately-paced song in 2/4 time.
Nigun (**niggun** or **nigun**) - means *melody* in both Yiddish and Hebrew, is a slow to mid-paced, melodious chant in 2/4 time.
Sher is a set dance in 2/4 time. It is one of the most common klezmer dances.
Sirba – a Romanian dance in 2/2 or 2/4 time.
Skotshne – can be either an instrumental display or dance piece.
Terkish (or **terk**) - a 4/4 dance like the habanera; in a Turkish style.

About the Author

As well as a musician, Johanna M Bolton is an author/illustrator who writes science fiction, mystery novels, and best-selling music books. She has also written textbooks including the GED books for Barron's Educational Series, fanzines, and features for newspapers. She is also the CEO of International Digital Book Publishing.

She lives in the woods with a pair of Australian Cattle Dogs and an ancient Shih Tzu who is possibly the reincarnation of a Chinese empress. "When I'm not working, painting, writing, or feeding someone," she said, "I play the fiddle and the mountain dulcimer. But, as always, everything in my life is subject to change at any time and without notice."

Other Music Books from Fat Pony Music

Celtic Fiddle
THE LITTLE BOOK OF IRISH FIDDLE TUNES
30 Irish tunes selected for the beginning and intermediate player. 5.5 x 8.5"

THE LITTLE BOOK OF SCOTTISH FIDDLE TUNES
30 Scottish tunes selected for the beginning and intermediate player. 5.5 x 8.5"

Mountain Dulcimer
FLAT-PICKING & FLATPICKING ON THE MOUNTAIN DULCIMER - 25 songs as well as instruction for all level players.

DULCIMER CHRISTMAS – A collection of 30 Traditional Christmas Carols arranged for a DAD tuned dulcimer.

Bowed Psaltery
20 CELTIC TUNES arranged for the Bowed Psaltery and other Treble Instruments. These are songs that may be familiar as well as some that are more obscure. 8.5 x 11"

EARLY MUSIC FOR THE BOWED PSALTERY is 30 musical pieces from the 13th to 17th centuries arranged for the bowed psaltery or other C instruments such as the recorder, penny whistle, or fiddle. This is European music from the Medieval, Renaissance, & Early Baroque periods. 8.5 x 11"

A PSALTERY CHRISTMAS - A collection of traditional Christmas carols spanning the centuries in Europe and the Americas. 8.5 x 11"

PLAY IT NOW! Easy Tunes for the Bowed Psaltery. This is a collection of easy songs for the beginning player with the number system developed by Jon Williams who not only makes psalteries, but also leads psaltery workshops at numerous festivals in the United States. The book can be used with or without the number system.

PLAY IT NOW II - Celtic Tunes for the Bowed Psaltery. A collection of easy Celtic tunes arranged with the Williams Number system. Like all the Psaltery music books, the tunes can be played on any treble instrument such as the recorder, penny whistle, or fiddle.

All books are available online from amazon.com
and other online vendors.

If you are interested in submitting your original manuscript to International Digital Book Publishing, Send a query to: fatponymusic52@yahoo.com

IDBPI publishes paper as well as digital books. Primarily a publisher of mainstream, mystery, science fiction, and fantasy novels, **20 CELTIC TUNES FOR THE BOWED PSALTERY** was their first venture into non-fiction publishing. Other titles can be found online through amazon.com and other online book distributers.

Professional book editing, formatting, and cover design is available as well.
visit https://johannambolton.com

www.ingramcontent.com/pod-product-compliance
Lightning Source LLC
LaVergne TN
LVHW051205080426
835508LV00021B/2827